Old DUNBAR

by

David Anderson

WE ARE ALL "DIGGING" AT DUNBAR THIS SUMMER.   NO. 121.

This happy family group captures the spirit of seaside holidays in the Edwardian period. A short trip to a resort like Dunbar was all many people could afford for their annual trip away from home, although a few wealthier visitors might consider leasing a villa for the summer season. The shops in the High Street could supply all that was needed, from buckets and spades to picnic sets and swimming costumes. The sender of this card 'had a splendid holiday here and everyone has enjoyed themselves. The weather throughout has been very good.'

1933.   JOHNSTONE'S CLOSE, DUNBAR.

© David Anderson 2000
First published in the United Kingdom, 2000,
by Stenlake Publishing, Ochiltree Sawmill, The Lade,
Ochiltree, Ayrshire, KA18 2NX
Telephone / Fax: 01290 423114
www.stenlake.co.uk

ISBN 1 84033 121 6

This postcard illustrates one of the more picturesque closes running off the High Street, which as the town's main business centre was – and is – lined with shops and tenements. Behind most of these, however, were a series of lesser dwellings, workshops, warehouses and stables connected by a passageway or 'close'. These often ran down one of the dividing walls separating each plot (such as the one on the left in this picture) and were open at both ends – most are recorded as 'common thoroughfares' in old records as they provided short cuts for pedestrians. The town council whitewashed the walls regularly, although the question of clearing drains and removing litter was often the subject of dispute between them and the landowners. Those that lived in the closes came up with ingenious means of coping with the cramped conditions; the washing hanging from the propped line is a good example.

INTRODUCTION

The images in this book chart Dunbar's heyday as a holiday resort and cover a period from about 1880 up until the years before the Second World War. Almost all of them are taken from picture postcards, and are just a selection of well over a thousand different cards published from the beginning of the twentieth century onwards (although many of the earliest postcards used older images). They look at Dunbar's tourist facilities, the pools and parks; its streets and hotels; and some of the more unusual images focus on the activities and portraits of local people.

Today it is difficult to appreciate the effects the annual influx of visitors had on both the prosperity of the town and also its physical layout. New streets were created to accommodate the growing aspirations of better off families in the town. The first of these ran along the East Links and was followed by another on part of the Kirkhill, which was feued off to become Bowmont Terrace. After that the focus switched to the West End with developments beyond Bayswell, including Mayville Park, Gardener Street, Letham Place and Marine Road (the latter consisting of properties almost exclusively used for summer lease). New hotels appeared, from the converted Roxburghe Lodge to new buildings such as the Bayswell and the town's flagship Bellevue Hotel, now sadly a (listed) ruin caught up in a redevelopment saga.

Businesses on the High Street prospered. There were several upmarket grocers and wine merchants who profited from steady summer trade from those who leased properties rather than staying in the hotels. Aitken the chemist began a profitable sideline in soft drinks (the lemonade works only closed in the 1970s) and many of the blacksmiths and coachbuilders benefited when carriage and coaching concerns branched out into bicycle and charabanc hire. Blacksmiths quickly adapted to the internal combustion engine in the early years of the twentieth century by opening garages and supplying fuel and mechanical expertise. The Stark family commenced a bus operation with daily summer tours from their base at the St George Hotel on the High Street.

The rise in tourism coincided with declines in the manpower necessary on local farms and a period of dearth in the local fishing industry, but fortunately new jobs were created in High Street businesses and the garages mentioned above. Fishermen turned their hands to coastal fishing trips for anglers and excursions 'around the bay'. They often ventured as far as the Bass Rock and May Island with parties of tourists. The more picturesque members of the community were always in

demand as photographic subjects and the local paper (the *Haddingtonshire Courier*) suggests that they were amenable to posing for a small consideration. In the inter-war years further decline in traditional employment was ameliorated by the application of Government grants towards infrastructure development – the great Bayswell Pool complex was a result of this scheme, and it lasted fifty years. Other less apparent benefits were increased water supplies cleaned by a new filtration works at Spott and new housing schemes for local residents because, particularly in the older quarter around the Shore, much of the existing housing stock was of poor standard and densely crowded. Another benefit was the spread and diversification of public entertainment and the arrival of cinemas.

Dunbar people had always 'entertained themselves' and amateur dramatics, debating and choral societies were well supported in the town. Although travelling shows regularly visited, local amateur entertainers petitioned the town council for licences to entertain summer visitors. By the 1920s professional troupes (always remembered as the Pierrots) were vying to play the pavilion in Winterfield Park. Returning to the early 1900s, an early 'kineomatic' entrepreneur showed movies (including the now lost *Launch of the Dunbar Lifeboat*) at a summer bazaar in Roxburghe Park and the Corn Exchange was soon leased for cinema projection. An old granary, the Dreadnought, became for a time the Argyll Theatre where cinema alternated with variety. By the late 1930s there were two purpose-built cinemas – the Empire in the High Street and the Playhouse, situated where the medical centre is today.

Dunbar had not always been a resort. Some of its military connections are mentioned in the following pages, but the town's real significance in historic times was its very location. It lies at what was a strategic site at the mouth of the Firth of Forth beside the rich arable lands of the Lothian Plain. A settlement near the castle existed more than 2,000 years ago, probably as a regional centre of the British tribe that the Romans called the Votadini. In their language Dunbar means 'fort on the height' or something similar, a phrase which well describes the castle headland.

Archaeology also shows that this fort became an Anglian stronghold when the Angles swept out of Northumbria and overran the native British of the Lothians. It is through Anglian accounts that, in AD 678, the town first enters written history. The life of Bishop Wilfrid recounts how, in that year, he was exiled to the 'King's vill of Dynbaer' under the supervision of the resident reeve, or royal officer. The town slips from view in succeeding centuries until 1072, when a descendant of the Northumbrian kings and cousin of Malcolm Canmore, one Gospatrick, was granted the lands of Dunbar (and much territory in the Borders besides). For a spell Gospatrick had been Earl of Northumberland, but having attached himself to the fortunes of the old English royal house (to whom he was also closely related) he had to flee the displeasure of William the Conqueror. Canmore installed his battle-hardened cousin as the principal magnate in south-eastern Scotland, an area outside the traditional Scottish heartlands and their established hierarchy where a loyal strongman was necessary for the territory's administration.

In the early twelfth century Gospatrick's son (also Gospatrick) was counted amongst the Earls of Scotland and his descendants held the title of Dunbar and March for another ten generations. Their number included warriors, several heroic countesses and crusaders, plus churchmen and poets. They put in their claim for Scotland's crown amongst the competitors of the late thirteenth century and finally overreached themselves against the Stewarts and their Douglas allies in the fifteenth century, when the family lost all their traditional lands.

The castle of Dunbar was always the heart of the earldom and its possession was critical to secure the flank of any invading force. Before the age of gunpowder it was reckoned impregnable, a fact exploited by the earls who sometimes supported England, sometimes Scotland (and often both at the same time), in the many periods of war between the two nations. Records survive of its development as a royal fortress. It was selected to house the royal artillery train and a very early artillery bastion is part of the surviving structure. The castle was caught up in the events surrounding the reign of Mary Queen of Scots and was eventually deliberately taken down and the remnants and site sold to a townsman.

The town of Dunbar is a legacy of the earldom. It was created a burgh to control local trade and gained in status when it was raised to a free burgh under the Crown in 1369. Its merchants and tradesmen elected a council to administer their affairs; this was finally abolished in 1975 under local government reorganisation and its place taken by a community council. The early council had draconian powers and regulated both trade and local behaviour through the magistrates court. Its members were elected by an arcane procedure that essentially stifled dissent and was wide open to abuse. It took until the early years of the nineteenth century to establish effective reforms and a degree of accountability to the ratepayers.

Situated in the shadow of the castle, the town had a troubled development. If the former was impregnable, the latter certainly was not, its wall serving only to control the streets at night and regulate imports. The result was frequently catastrophic for the inhabitants. Dunbar was put to the torch several times and several major battles were fought nearby. Even in the eighteenth century, long after it might be thought safe, it had to juggle between the arrival (and prompt departure) of Hanoverian forces and then a Jacobite occupation. However, that same century was generally a time of prosperity and rising population. Several trading fortunes were made (and several others lost) on industrial ventures.

The nineteenth century was a period of mixed fortunes. Many families emigrated to look for new opportunities in the British colonies and the New World (many families in Dunbar are still in touch with relatives overseas), prompted in part by changing economic conditions at home. For those that remained there were increasing opportunities. Extensions to the franchise even meant that women could vote in council elections (providing they owned sufficient property in their own right). Money was spent on improving the town's infrastructure, with new schools, running water, gas lamps to light the streets, the new Victoria Harbour, turnpikes to speed road connections and the railway to add another dimension to travel. The last part of the century brought the first rush of tourists and the town expanded even more to cater for them. It was a boom that lasted almost a hundred years.

Tourism still plays an important part in the local economy, although its nature has changed over the years. There are proposals to develop a new visitor centre around John Muir's birthplace, currently a small museum, thus tapping into current trends in environmental awareness and playing to strengths in Dunbar's location. Several other proposals have been made to develop new golf courses and golfing tourism is on the rise over the whole county. With these and other initiatives, such as the success of the Town House Museum over the last few years, it is to be expected that tourism will continue to play its part in Dunbar.

Most of the pictures on the following pages were picked by visitors to Dunbar who chose them as souvenirs or posted them to their friends back home; many have messages on the back that describe the highlights of their holiday. This is their chance to be enjoyed again.

Ruins of Watergate,
('Where Mary Queen of Scots escaped from Dunbar Castle.)

Dunbar Castle once ranked as one of Scotland's greatest, having been home for over 300 years to the powerful Anglo-Celtic Earls of Dunbar, descended from Malcolm Canmore's cousin Gospatrick. When the family fell from favour, the castle was taken for the Crown. It was deliberately destroyed in 1568: the Scottish Government was anxious to placate Elizabeth of England and ensure there was nowhere which might stand against James VI when he inherited her throne.

The castle is probably Dunbar's oldest structure. Its ruin sits on a headland, surrounded by cliffs. This very early photograph was taken around 1868 before the fragment of wall with the arch fell during a storm. The wall was all that remained of the castle's great hall and was marked with heraldic carvings dating to the late fourteenth century. These had probably been installed by George, the tenth Earl of Dunbar, to record his family's possession of the earldoms of March, Moray and the Isle of Man – the greatest extent of their lands. His son was to lose nearly everything because by 1440 the Crown and the Douglas family had combined to ruin the Dunbars' fortunes.

New Harbour and Castle, Dunbar

The main pier of the Victoria Harbour was designed to handle coastal freighters. However the opening of the harbour was coincident with the development of the railway system and as a result it never experienced the commercial traffic that had been expected. Most of what there was was agriculturally-related, with feedstocks and fertilisers being imported and potatoes, grain and spirits from East Linton's distillery forming the main export traffic. Behind the masts of the ship there is a huddle of buildings under the shelter of the castle: this was a pioneering fisheries research station. Some of the methods developed there are still used by fish farms today. The Victoria Harbour's north pier (part of which lies on the right of this photograph) was a popular place for summer strolls with Dunbar's visitors. There was always something to see, and the more adventurous could climb the wall for breathtaking views or simply sit in the sunshine watching the activity all around. The far end, by the harbour mouth, was popular with anglers.

The Castle Rock closes the west end of the Victoria Harbour; it was only by blasting away the rock's northerly portion that an acceptable entrance to the harbour was created. This led to the loss of much of the castle's encircling wall as well as its seaward towers, the preservation of which were not a priority to the Victorian harbour builders. The passage of time and landward development have reduced the surviving fragments even more, so that what stands is a bare reflection of past glories. The height of the rock, to the right of the high stack, has long been favoured as a lookout point and beacon-site. It was last used when a fire was lit to mark the passage of 1999 and the start of a new millennium.

DUNBAR CASTLE AND HARBOUR

B 9804

The battery on Lammer Island (foreground) never fired a shot in anger. It was built in the late eighteenth century in response to two raids by privateers – John Paul Jones appeared off the town on a foray up the North Sea and another less official American, Captain Fall, ventured near the town in the same period. The latter was described as a noted pirate; however he shared an uncommon surname with Dunbar's leading family so perhaps there was an element of personal or family animosity involved.

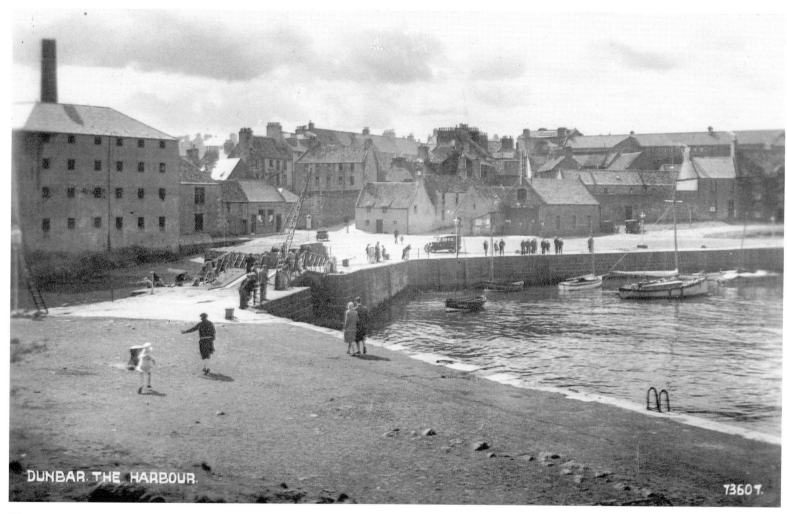

DUNBAR. THE HARBOUR.

7360 T.

The town's roofline forms a pleasing view when looking from Lammer Island back towards the mainland. The granary and lifeboat house provide constant features in this view where almost all of the other buildings have been demolished or renovated over the years. These buildings contained most of the pubs, shops, stores and boats' chandlers around the harbours, and their replacements give an altogether more gentrified feel to the area today.

Dunbar was a garrison town from the Napoleonic period until after the Second World War. For a substantial proportion of this time the headquarters of the East Lothian Yeomanry Cavalry (later the Lothians and Border Horse) were maintained at the barracks and militia artillery volunteers paraded in the volunteer hall, now the Royal British Legion clubhouse. This photograph shows a group of artillery volunteers at a live firing exercise on the Castle Park headland. The volunteers were trained to serve as garrison artillery, so it didn't matter that their guns were mostly superannuated naval pieces. When the guns were eventually replaced, some of them were retained in Dunbar to decorate clifftop parkland.

These guns, situated in Bayswell Park, had been used by the volunteer artillery forces that formerly mustered in Dunbar for summer exercises. They remained at Bayswell until the Second World War. Where they then went is something of a mystery – some say they were melted down for the war effort, but another rumour suggests that they were buried to prevent that happening.

This group photograph shows NCOs and other ranks of the Haddingtonshire Artillery Volunteers, a unit that became part of the South-east Scotland Militia Artillery. Many of the NCOs were retired regulars with immense experience of service. They were responsible for the year-round training of the men and led live firing exercises in the summer. It was the disbanding of this unit in 1907 – when the volunteers and militia were integrated into the new Territorial Army – that prompted the building of a new barracks block alongside Lauderdale House and the posting of a regular cavalry brigade to Dunbar.

LAUDERDALE HOUSE, CAVALRY BARRACKS, DUNBAR

A southerly view of Lauderdale House with the High Street directly behind it. The central block of the house was commissioned by Captain James Fall in the early eighteenth century. A wealthy entrepreneur, he wanted a dwelling to reflect his status as MP in the Scottish and later United Kingdom parliaments. His son sold the property to the Earl of Lauderdale who had the building remodelled by James Adam; this involved adding the wings and colonnaded portico. When the military purchased the property in the mid-nineteenth century, its garden was levelled for a parade ground. The house became a barracks, and volunteer artillery regiments mustered there for live firing practice. Newspapers of the period record dances, military sports, parades and all the bustle of a garrison town. The site continued as a military base through both World Wars and, long after the military departed, the near derelict Lauderdale House was redeveloped as apartments.

Cats' Row, Dunbar

The Cats Row was a collection of picturesque old tenements in the lower part of Victoria Street. Most of the apartments were rented to fisher families, as they were conveniently located for harbour users. The whole area has been redeveloped – the buildings were condemned as slums in the 1930s – and their loss has meant a certain decline in the character of the approaches to the harbours. It also led to the dispersal of the fishing community to the new housing estates at Parson's Pool and the Boroughdales.

This old alley disappeared when Victoria Street was redeveloped. It ran from Castle Gate, past the back of the Cats Row on the right and the side of Shore Hall on the left, to the Broadhaven. The Shore Hall was at the heart of the fishing community; it was used for wedding parties and entertainment and was the base of a mission sponsored by the local churches. The 'midden', beside the child on the left, was a feature of every close or pend. The town council gained revenue from the lease of the town's 'dung', which was collected by scavenger carts and used for fertiliser after composting.

APPROACH TO BEACH, DUNBAR.

The foot of Silver Street is only a hundred yards from the sea at the East Beach. The tenement in the centre of the picture is long gone, the site occupied today by a piece of rough ground and a small amusement park. The house marked the entrance to Colvin Street, a made-up name replacing the earlier 'Coffin Street', which was discarded by a Victorian committee keen to tidy up unseemly matters for the benefit of visitors. Several other places were renamed at the same time, a process that continues today as new developments are created on regenerated sites.

Dunbar's fine, wide High Street was regularly used for public celebrations and local fairs, and windows looking over the street from the mixture of eighteenth, nineteenth and twentieth century tenements often provided vantage points to watch the stir in the road. This picture shows the east side of the High Street looking south to the Free Kirk at its terminus. The buildings are a heterogeneous mixture. The one on the extreme left shows that the oldest were built with their gable ends facing the street and a gap to allow passage to the backlands or closes. Most of the buildings in that style (including the one in the picture) have now fallen victim to redevelopment, but a careful look at some of the older surviving properties reveals that their roofs have been remodelled to conform with those of their neighbours. The High Street was lit by gas around the start of the twentieth century. Most of the lampposts were made locally at Dunbar Foundry, located where the Eden Hotel is today, and the gas was generated at a site a few hundred yards along the Belhaven Road.

The caption on this postcard reads: 'Draft of Lanarkshire Yeomanry leaving Dunbar'. The town's military connections threw it into the First World War with immediate effect. At first, units of the Territorial Army were mustered in Dunbar in preparation for mobilisation with the British Expeditionary Force in France. As the war went on, new recruits and recovered wounded assembled in the town until there were sufficient to form a draft. When their orders came the men and their officers marched down the centre of the High Street from the barracks to the railway station.

The town council and their staff parade along the High Street, on their way to church shortly after the annual burgh elections. They were about to celebrate the 'kirking of the council', a service to solemnise their authority. Ceremony was also important when new councillors took their oaths of allegiance to the Crown. Some took the opportunity to be created burgesses at the same time; this required swearing to defend the rights of the burgh under arms, and shouldering an old musket whilst doing so to show willing. Even the police got involved, by 'tabling their batons' before the provost in a ceremonial reminder of the days when their authority stemmed solely from the council. By placing their batons, a symbol of office, on the table, constables acknowledged the council's right to approve or disapprove them keeping their jobs.

This photograph captures a fair proportion of Dunbar's population as a parade, led by the town band, wends its way up the High Street. It's hard to know what the occasion was, but the picture can be dated to after 1908 by the presence of the Scout Troop (third contingent in the parade). Judging by the sombre clothes, the event might have been the death of King Edward VII. Whatever is depicted, the image gives some idea of the usefulness of the street for civic events; the far part continued to be regularly closed in the summer for public entertainment until the 1970s.

...emaly...a...of Dunbar...in Parish Church.

George Home of Spott began a meteoric political career by securing the position of Provost of Dunbar around November 1600 (he was probably the town's first provost). Five years later his patron, James VI, created him Earl of Dunbar and he rose to become Lord High Treasurer of Scotland. He stepped on toes during his rise and made further enemies by advocating the return of bishops to the Presbyterian Church. Home died in London in mysterious circumstances (the rumour was that he was poisoned) and was brought back to Dunbar to be buried in the parish church, where this wonderful Italianate tomb was erected over his resting-place. The tomb has survived both the replacement of the church around it and a serious fire of some years ago. It was carefully restored, but still bears the scars of the fire.

Dunbar's Free Church was built at the end of the High Street in the 1840s on the site of the town's bowling green. This long-established green had occupied the same spot since medieval buildings were cleared from it in the eighteenth century. Following the building of the church, a new green was laid out in what became Station Road, a convenient location for catching the attention of the town's visitors, most of who arrived by train. In the Edwardian period weekly, monthly and season tickets were available for a few shillings. The partners of active participants could enjoy fine views from the perimeter gardens while their spouses played a game of bowls.

Roxburghe Marine Hotel, DUNBAR

Converted from a rather grand estate lodge, the former home of a dowager duchess, the Roxburghe Marine Hotel offered Edwardian holidaymakers all the modern luxuries they desired. Its speciality was therapeutic baths, which were supplied with water from the nearby sea, although it also had its own bathing place along the East Links. Once, the many staff included a professional masseur. The Roxburghe was conveniently placed for the popular East Beach, where a fine stretch of sand was exposed at low tide and there were a variety of kiosks selling gifts and snacks. The hotel was demolished in the 1990s to make way for a proposed housing development.

215 The Cottages, Dunbar

The Cottages were built speculatively at the townward end of the East Links during the early years of the nineteenth century. They were joined by another block in Victorian times. Both developments had a service lane that ran between the homes and their gardens. Most of the houses provided access directly onto the beach via ladders and steps from the sea wall. As a consequence, they were popular rental properties with holiday visitors; an added attraction was that the East Links Beach was generally quieter than the nearby East Beach.

The Railway Inn was one of Dunbar's oldest hostelries and predated the opening of the line between Edinburgh and Berwick in 1846, at which point it adopted its new name. The inn's clientele were mostly drawn from commercial travellers and country folk with business in the town. It had a reputation for extended opening hours, and in the days when only 'genuine travellers' could purchase alcoholic refreshment on Sundays the Railway frequently featured in the magistrates' court in disputes over the definition of 'genuine'. Just in shot to the left of the picture is the Royal Hotel, newly built to cater for summer visitors and commanding a good situation between the station and High Street.

Cleik-im-in Toll stood at a crossroads on the routes from Dunbar to Spott and Broxburn to Belton. The tollkeeper's cottage disappeared long ago under the tarmac of the A1. It was used for many years to collect charges from road-users under the Turnpike Trusts Act, the revenues being applied to road making and maintenance. In the year 2000 a new roundabout was opened on this site as the highway was being prepared for further widening and upgrading.

Cleikimin Toll, near Dunbar.

This curious sandstone tower stands in the field of Friar's Croft steading, and is now surrounded by a supermarket car park. Clearly once part of a larger building, it is lined inside with nesting boxes and known locally as The Doocot, from its former use as a pigeon loft. It was once the belfry and core of a Trinitarian Friary church founded by an Earl of Dunbar and endowed by his Countess when he went on crusade to the Holy Land. All the other parts of the church have been reused, having been dismantled and robbed out over the centuries. Archaeological investigations before development revealed the lines of walls, tiled floors and a graveyard.

BELHAVEN SANDS, DUNBAR

D 1146

The 'Bridge to Nowhere' gives low-tide access to the mile-long strand of Belhaven Bay. On the shoreward side, the sand is rather gritty, with many pebbles. However, just across the Beil Water, acres of safe, golden sand provide a child's delight. In the distance is the Bass Rock, one of Dunbar's more famous landmarks and home of a famed colony of gannets, many of which plummet for fish in the bay. At night, the lighthouse lamp provides the finishing touch to its beetle-like profile. This shore was once designated the port of Dunbar, where trading craft could be safely beached.

TENNIS COURTS AND PAVILIONS, PUBLIC PARK, DUNBAR. 98638. J.V.

Winterfield Park was developed during the late 1920s with a mixture of public and private finance. The land was donated anonymously but the park housed public facilities such as putting greens, sports pitches and, of course, the municipal tennis courts. In the distance behind the gates is the Pierrots' Pavilion, which later became the amenities block for Winterfield Caravan Park. Revenues from the activities in the park were used for its maintenance, and surplus cash was devoted to the town's common good fund. Winterfield once provided the perfect venue for day trippers who arrived by special excursion trains; the visitors were often over a thousand strong, and marched from the station through the town to the park.

This summer scene was recorded around 1935 in Winterfield Park during Dunbar's annual gala. A large crowd has gathered to watch local children dance around a maypole set near the park's pavilion. The pavilion was built to provide a venue for Pierrot entertainers, and the stage that the entertainers used can be seen below the balcony. Around the perimeter were shelters; the park lies close to the cliffs on the west and has a rather exposed situation. The hardy visitors attracted by Dunbar's 'bracing easterly breezes' sometimes found them a bit too much!

The Zenith Entertainers (photographed in 1925) were one of several groups to appear at Dunbar in the 1920s and 1930s. Despite their official name, everybody knew them as the Pierrots. The entertainers performed on an open-air stage at the pavilion in front of a fenced compound. It cost a small amount to sit, but anyone could see the show for free by standing outside. This postcard was produced as part of the troupe's publicity material – at the close of the show, the performers would quickly circulate amongst the crowd selling cards and signing autographs.

This tide-swamped gully was the gentlemen's bathing pond, or 'old bathe' (the name that was being used in the middle of the nineteenth century). At the beginning of the twentieth century, male bathers were relegated to this site and another similar spot on the east of the town lest the sight of them cause consternation to the sensibilities of 'lady bathers' (or vice versa). The sandy pool was ideal for learning to swim and beyond, on the rocks, a path and steps admitted the adventurous to the open sea for more challenging exercise.

LADIES' BATHING PAVILION, DUNBAR.

The ladies' bathing pavilion was perched precariously above the waves on stone piles. The 'pond' lay below the waves on the right. Until the 1920s it really only consisted of a shallow scrape in the rocks with a low retaining wall to hold back some water. However, at low tide it provided a relatively safe play area for children and, exclusively for many years, their mothers. Men and older boys were consigned to other bathing places, and had to keep well away from the area surrounding the 'ladies' bathe'.

30

832. SWIMMING POOL, DUNBAR.

The construction of the 'Safety Swimming Pond' in the 1920s marked the culmination of a sequenced development programme that equipped the town with a comprehensive modern bathing complex. The new pond was built on the site of the old Victorian pool (the former women's pool), but there was no real comparison. It held 500,000 gallons of filtered sea water, was 75 by 50 yards and had an Olympic-class diving pit. With a ballroom, plentiful indoor changing facilities, a canteen, and a curving swathe of terraced spectator accommodation, the pond was an immediate hit: summer galas could attract 5,000 paying visitors.

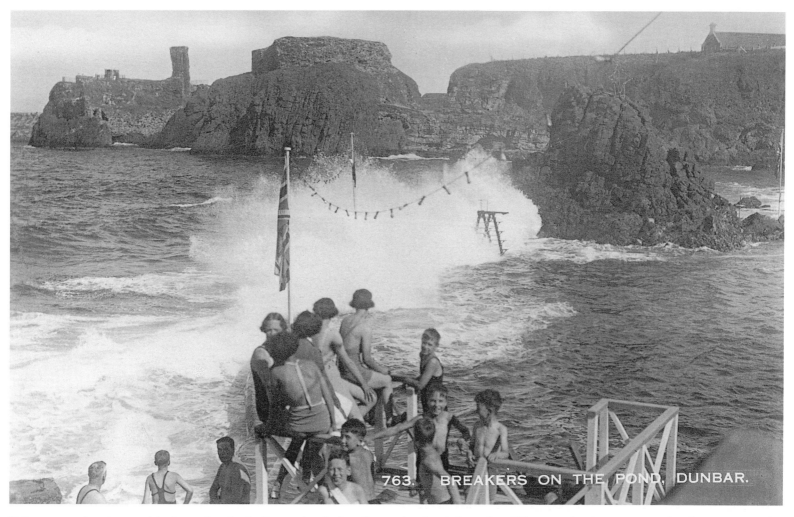

763. BREAKERS ON THE POND, DUNBAR.

If the new swimming pool had one drawback, it was that its location under the shelter of a cliff meant that it was exposed to heavy seas. This photograph, taken on a stormy summer's day, shows the waves breaking on the pond's (hidden) sea wall, although the prospect for swimming must have been quite good judging by the number of people perched on the superstructure of the slides. The picture also gives a good idea of the scenic qualities of the pond, with the Castle Park cliffs and Castle Rock in the background.

When the waves weren't sweeping in over the sea wall the new swimming pool proved remarkably popular, as this quite astonishing photograph illustrates. It was taken in the early 1930s and shows the crowd arranged all over and around the pond's diving board and spring boards. In the pool's first few years of operation yearly profits came in at several thousand pounds (at a time when £100 was an average annual working wage). This bounty for the town's funds came from entrance tickets, special events such as galas and dances, and the franchises let out by the council.

This atmospheric photograph was taken from the pier of the Old or Cromwell Harbour. Generally relegated to the status of a quiet backwater following the opening of the New (Victoria) Harbour, it is still useful in stormy weather as it can be more sheltered. The shore-side frontage was once made up of a mixture of commercial and residential properties, many of which have been redeveloped in recent years. The three-storey mansion was owned by Christopher Middlemass, who dominated Dunbar's business and political community in the early nineteenth century. He awaited the return of his ships from trading ventures in the Mediterranean and Americas from this house. For a long time the entrances of both the Old and Victoria Harbours were provided with a set of booms, which could be quickly lowered into sockets to form a wall during stormy conditions.

A host of fishing boats crowd into the Old Harbour, perhaps to shelter against a storm predicted by the weatherglass on the Fishermen's Monument (see page 37). A number of the boats have partially hoisted their sails, or draped them over their lowered masts. As the sails were made from canvas they were susceptible to rot if stored damp. The council provided a 'barking house' where new sails could be boiled (for a charge) in a solution obtained from the bark of tropical trees. This gave them some protection against deterioration, but also dyed them dark brown.

A hundred years ago fishing was a family affair. Men and boys went to sea and their wives, sisters and daughters prepared their lines. This was an essential task, as each line had hundreds of hooks that needed to be baited using shelled mussels (and sometimes limpets) before being laid out in a skul – a wicker basket designed so that the line could be cast without snaring or tangling the hooks. Once landed, some of the catch might be smoked or salted; this group has been posed in front of a small smokehouse. In Victorian times and earlier the fish might have been hawked around the town by girls such as these. Some of the earliest ordinances of the burgh (surviving from the sixteenth century) relate to the sale of fish.

Custom House Square lies between the Broadhaven and the Old Harbour; it has been completely redeveloped since this photograph was taken. The Georgian custom house (whose doorway is shown on the right here) was the headquarters of a team of officers and men who collected a whole variety of taxes. They were assisted by officers of the Preventative Service who searched for contraband goods, with a boat for intercepting traffic at sea. For a time in the nineteenth century the coastguard service was based in the building, but it was latterly used as low-cost housing, leased mainly to members of the fishing community.

Around the harbours was an area made up of old tenements, warehouses, workshops and yards linked by narrow wynds and passageways. This one ran between Writer's Court and Victoria Street, where the entrance was beside the Volunteer Arms public house. Cats, such as the two in this picture, were a feature of the Shore for many years. Most of them were not domesticated, but were semi-wild feral hunters that were tolerated because they usefully kept down vermin. Their other source of food was fish scraps, which could be found in plenty wherever a fisherman had been working.

The fishermen's monument at Cromwell Harbour provided a wonderful prop for Edwardian postcard photographers, and several of the denizens of the harbour appear in more than one of the cards they produced. The real purpose of the plinth was to house a public barometer: it was located in the cabinet above the sitting figure. This was an important facility when it was erected in 1856, because few fishermen could afford their own barometers. It meant that local weather knowledge could be backed up with accurate data, which indirectly helped to save lives.

This Edwardian photograph shows two Dunbar fishing yawls loaded practically to the gunwales with herring. The image gives a good idea of the cramped conditions aboard open fishing boats: there is little room for the catch, let alone the crew and their equipment. These boats were used mainly for working near the shore, staying out at most overnight. Most had a crew of three or four, who had the wearisome task of rowing themselves home on occasions when there was no wind. Dunbar's fishermen and their yawls, mostly using long lines (netting being reserved for the herring run), came under severe pressure from large English and Continental steam drifters in the early part of the twentieth century. Many men barely scraped a living from the sea and some were forced to seek alternative work.

Bob Marr, the young man on the right of this picture, became one of the most well-known inhabitants of Dunbar's harbours. He worked on his creels on the pier beside the castle ruins most days, and when this photograph was taken he was accompanied by Tom Pat Johnson and James Tear. All three men were from long-established fishing families, where son followed father to sea. The picture records one of the daily chores of the trade, mending and refurbishing lobster pots. Weather conditions frequently caused a high rate of attrition and lost creels were, and still are, commonplace.

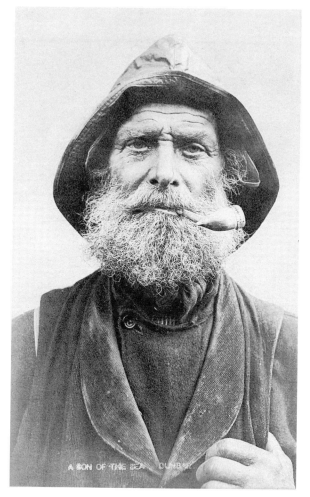

These two portrait postcards are part of a remarkable and unusual series by Francis Sanson of Dunbar. They serve as striking reminders of the town's debt to the local fishing community, whose way of life was often passed from father to son. The fishermen's job was hazardous in the extreme, with accounts of drowning and lost boats a regular feature of the nineteenth century. In addition to danger, the work was often ill-rewarded and subject to cycles of plenty and dearth, with frequent competition for fishing grounds. Descendants of these men still live in the town today, although few still make their living from the sea.

The world famous gannet colony on the Bass Rock has been drawing visitors with ornithological interests since tourism began. Early visitors to this part of the world were always treated to a dish made with the meat of the bird; current generations make do with inspecting their precipitous nests from boats, as landing is still controlled by the proprietors and the Rock is now a nature reserve. It is planned to install remote video cameras to bring the domestic life of the seabirds to screens in the new Scottish Seabird Centre at North Berwick.

Lighthouse-keeping was supposed to be lonely work, but with one of Britain's great natural sights on their doorstep the keepers on the Bass Rock enterprisingly worked up a little sideline by selling picture postcards to tourists ferried out to the island. This card was bought there in 1922, and gives some idea of how every suitable nesting site is quickly filled by the island's birds. In the near left corner a single egg sits in a nest of dried seaweed.

This stretch of water is the Broadhaven. The rock in the background is Lammer Island, with its pier, fort and hospital; on the right is a narrow channel leading eastwards to the open sea, one of the two available from the harbours. When the wind was from the correct direction, fishing yawls could sail straight out. But they had to beware because, in certain conditions, gusts from around the pier of the island had been known to catch sails and overset boats. In eventualities such as an upset, the lifeboat was only a few hundred yards away; its boathouse is still at the head of the Broadhaven. It is seen here exercising on Lifeboat Day, the main fund-raising event for the service. At Dunbar, lifeboat days were inaugurated át the rededication of the *Wallace* in the 1880s and have continued in almost unbroken succession since. However, the present boats only have one option on launching, that of leaving the harbour to the west. When the New Harbour wall was repaired in the 1960s, the rubble was used to close the Broadhaven channel, which helped to shelter the harbours but left only the narrow western entrance navigable.

" William Arthur Millward ". DUNBAR LIFEBOAT entering the harbour after rendering istanc to a vessel in distress.

Dunbar's first lifeboat was bought in 1808 and was funded by the county with the intention of providing a necessary service. It failed through a combination of accident, the hijacking of the assets to other ends, and neglect in the absence of a training programme. It was ahead of its time, however, and some of the lessons learnt were incorporated in the organisation of what became the Royal National Lifeboat Institution. RNLI lifeboats have been stationed at Dunbar since the 1860s. There have been many successful rescues, but the lifeboat volunteers have undertaken a dangerous calling: even returning to base can be difficult, as this image shows.

The wreck of the Norwegian steamer *Prosum* on the Thorntonloch shore was a golden opportunity for local photographer Francis Sanson to take a memorable picture. The *Prosum* went ashore during the night of 24 October 1908. Her crew took to their boats and were quickly rescued by Dunbar's No. 2 lifeboat, the *Sarah Kay*. The ship was not so fortunate – this was the view a week after the stranding, shortly before man took over from the waves and the remains of the vessel were broken up for scrap.

Mr Browning (second right) and staff in the yard of his wheelwright's and blacksmithing business. The workers are all carrying the tools of their trades, many of them made by themselves as part of their training; three of them also have heavy leather aprons to protect their trousers. In the background there are a variety of iron tyres. These were heated to redness before being shrunk onto the wooden wheels of carts and carriages. Like its competitors, this yard looked for new products as technology changed, and later went into the manufacture of bicycles.

The streets around the Shore were once home to a good number of workshops and other small-scale industrial enterprises. Hugh White's joinery and coachbuilding firm was established in 1885 and adapted very well over the years to changing technology and the arrival of motor transport. The firm's skilled employees were eventually able to provide customers with purpose-built vehicles assembled on pre-purchased chassis. The new trades of mechanic and engineer found a place alongside traditional wheelwrights and coachbuilders. Senior employees passed on their knowledge to a new generation of apprentices who became the garage owners and staff of the next generation.

This photograph of an informal catch inspection was taken by the landward pier of Victoria Harbour. The only identified figure is the tall gentleman on the left. James Brand was an auctioneer by profession and was first elected to the town council in 1873, an appointment that marked the start of a remarkable career. In 1876 he was elected provost and served as such for an unbroken 20 year period; he was still a bailie in 1909. No-one else has come close to this record. The fisherman on the right is clad in a sou'wester and oilskin gaiters, and has arm protectors over his knitted jersey. James Brand also appears in the other picture on this page.

Two of Dunbar's Edwardian politicians and businessmen, Provosts Brand and Smith, are photographed in conversation with an engineer outside the Lorne Hotel in the High Street. The building on the left was the childhood home of East Lothian's 'Man of the Millennium', John Muir, in the 1840s. Muir is becoming increasingly well-known in Scotland for his pioneering work in conservation in the United States. His birthplace has been converted into a small museum, and was recently purchased by a community trust. Another trust has been prominent in the purchase of several estates for conservation purposes, working to Muir's principles.